FLIGHTLESS BIRDS

PICTURE LIBRARY

FLIGHTLESS BIRDS

Norman Barrett

Franklin Watts

New York   London   Sydney   Toronto

Library of Congress Cataloging-in-Publication Data

Barrett, Norman S.
    Flightless birds/Norman Barrett.
        p. cm. — (Picture library)
    Includes index.
    Summary: Examines the physical features, nesting, and feeding
    habits of several flightless birds, including the ostrich, rhea,
    emu, and cassowary.
    ISBN 0-531-14112-8
    1. Flightless birds — Juvenile literature. [1. Flightless birds
    2. Birds] I. Title. II. Series
QL676.2.B36 1990
598'.5—dc20   90-42382
                                                          CIP
                                                           AC

Designed by
Barrett and Weintroub

Research by
Deborah Spring

Picture Research by
Ruth Sonntag

Photographs by
Survival Anglia
N.S. Barrett Collection
New Zealand Wildlife Service

© 1991 Franklin Watts

Franklin Watts, Inc.
387 Park Avenue South
New York NY 10016

Illustration by
Rhoda and Robert Burns

Technical Consultant
Michael Chinery

Contents

Introduction

Not all birds can fly. Birds are the only animals with feathers, and all birds have wings. Most species (kinds) of birds can fly. Those that cannot are called flightless birds.

Among the best known flightless birds are ostriches and emus. These are big birds with long legs, who can run fast over the ground. Penguins are also flightless. They move speedily through the water.

△ A flock of wild ostriches speed over the open spaces of Etosha salt pan in Africa. Ostriches are the largest of all birds and the fastest over the ground.

The ancestors of today's flightless birds used to be able to fly, millions of years ago. They lost the power of flight because they had few natural enemies. They were able to live on the ground without the need to escape to the air or fly to find their food.

In most other respects, flightless birds are like other kinds of birds. They have two legs and two wings, they have a beak but no teeth, and they hatch from eggs.

△ Macaroni and chinstrap penguins on an island in Antarctica. Penguins spend most of their time in the water, but gather on land to make their nests and breed.

Looking at flightless birds

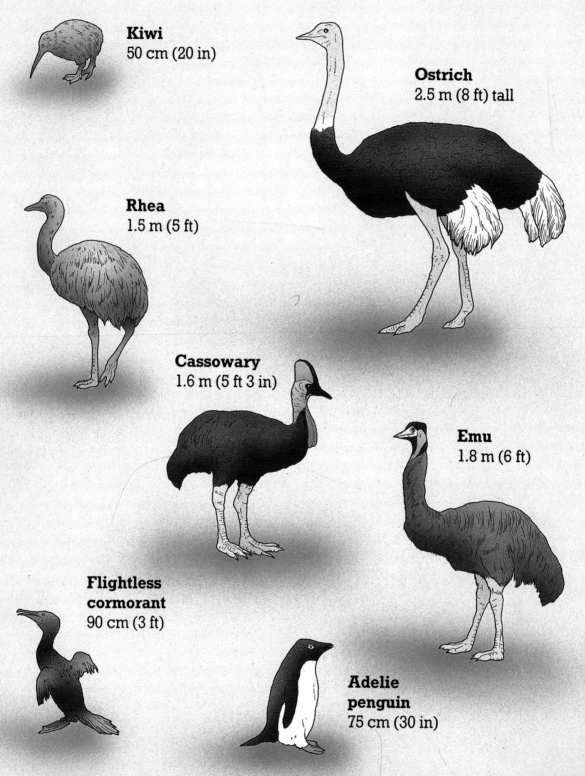

Kiwi
50 cm (20 in)

Ostrich
2.5 m (8 ft) tall

Rhea
1.5 m (5 ft)

Cassowary
1.6 m (5 ft 3 in)

Emu
1.8 m (6 ft)

Flightless cormorant
90 cm (3 ft)

Adelie penguin
75 cm (30 in)

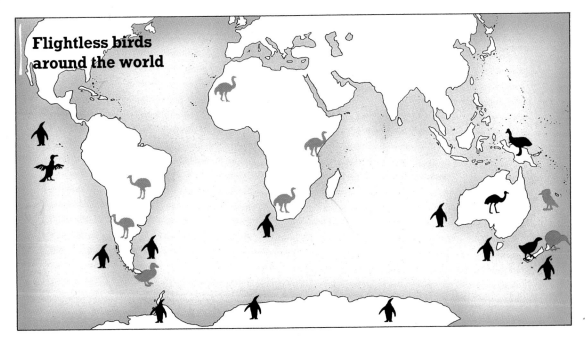

Flightless birds around the world

△ Flightless birds are found mainly in the southern half of the world.

▽ Feet – flightless birds have developed powerful feet to propel them along and to use as weapons when they defend themselves against predators.

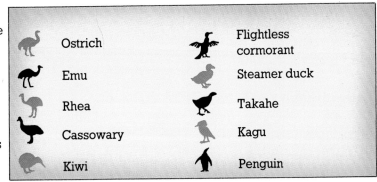

Ostrich		Flightless cormorant
Emu		Steamer duck
Rhea		Takahe
Cassowary		Kagu
Kiwi		Penguin

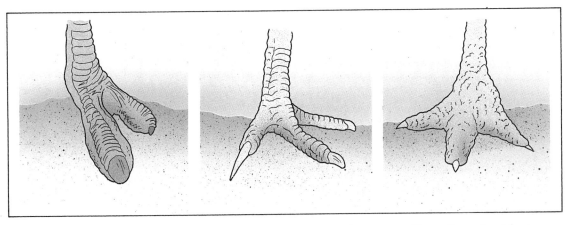

Ostrich – strong two-toed foot that is almost a hoof, with thick curved claws.

Cassowary – three-toed foot with long sharp claw on the inner toe, a dangerous weapon.

Emu – three-toed foot typical of most flightless birds.

9

Kinds of flightless birds

The ostrich, emu, cassowary and rhea are the largest of all living birds. All are fast runners with long necks and legs. Kiwis and penguins are much smaller, belonging to different groups with no close relatives.

A few species of flightless birds occur in other groups, but they do not look much different from their relatives. The steamer duck looks much like other ducks, and the flightless cormorant looks like any other cormorant.

▷The emu is an Australian bird. It lives wild in scrub and grasslands. Emus are regarded as pests because they eat crops.

◁The greater rhea, one of the two species of rhea. Rheas live in grasslands and open brush country in South America. Their feathers are used as dusters.

◁The long neck of the ostrich.

▷The cassowary lives in tropical forests, usually singly or in pairs.

▽The kiwi is a shy, nocturnal bird found only in New Zealand. It lives in the humid forests, where it roots around for worms, insects and fallen fruits with its long beak.

△ A flightless cormorant hangs its wings out to dry after fishing in the water. It lives only on the coasts of the Galapagos Islands, in the Pacific, where just a few hundred pairs exist.

◁ The majestic emperor penguin of Antarctica.

△ A pair of flightless steamer ducks perch on a rocky shore. These birds live on southern South American coasts. They use their short wings in diving and when moving swiftly across the water.

▷ The takahe is a large flightless swamphen of New Zealand. It was thought to be extinct until rediscovered on the shores of a mountain lake in 1948.

On land

The larger flightless birds are able to survive on the ground because they are either too big or too fast for their enemies. They have powerful legs and pack quite a kick. Cornered cassowaries have been known to kill people.

The ostrich and rhea rove about in flocks of up to 50 birds, often in the company of grazing animals. The males have several mates, who lay their eggs in the same nest.

▷ An ostrich at the nest with eggs and a chick. Like the other big birds, the ostrich scoops out a nest in the ground, and incubates the eggs (keeps them warm) if necessary.

▽ Emus drinking at a watering hole. Emus are not popular with Australian farmers because they compete with grazing cattle for grass and they tear down fences.

▷Ostriches in a national park in Southern Africa, in the company of wildebeest, a kind of antelope. Ostriches often travel with these and other grazing animals, such as zebra, who have common enemies – lions and other predators.

The two groups may be of benefit to each other. The ostriches, with their great height and keen eyesight, can alert their four-footed companions to danger. The grazing animals flush out food for the ostriches, who enjoy insects and other small animals as well as their usual diet of plants, seeds and fruit.

17.31940

Baby ostriches leave the nest within 24 hours and travel in "coveys" with the adults. At four weeks, they can run as fast as an adult. Ostriches can live for as long as 70 years.

Young rheas also leave the nest early, and reach full size in five months. Baby cassowaries are fed and protected by their father for about seven weeks. Young emus leave the nest soon after hatching, but may stay with their father for as long as 18 months.

△ A covey of ostrich chicks keep pace with their father in an African national park, with a young springbok nearby.

In water

Penguins are perfectly suited to the water, where they get all their food. What used to be wings are now flippers, which power them through the water as if they were flying.

They live only in the southern oceans, and breed on coasts and islands and on the ice of Antarctica. A breeding colony, or rookery, may consist of a million or more penguins.

▽ King penguins going down to the sea off South Georgia, an island near Antarctica. The 16 or so species of penguins lay their eggs and raise their young on land. They are not fast movers on land, walking with a clumsy, waddling motion. But they have few enemies.

◁ A king penguin incubates its egg between its feet and belly feathers. The male and female take turns to incubate, while the other goes to sea to bring back food.

▽ Penguins can move faster on ice and snow by "tobogganing," using their flippers as paddles.

The only other flightless seabirds are the cormorants of the Galapagos. Their wings are not useful as flippers, but they use their powerful legs for swimming.

Flightless steamer ducks use their wings to help them move quickly on the water. With a lot of flapping and a great deal of spray, they speed across the surface at up to 20 km/h (12 mph).

Rheas, cassowaries and emus are all strong swimmers.

▽ A pair of flightless cormorants nesting on a rocky Galapagos coast.

In captivity

Birds of the flightless type are, of course, the easiest to keep in captivity because they do not have to be confined in cages.

Ostriches, once farmed for their decorative plumes, are now raised for their skins, to make leather. Rheas do well in zoos and the young are kept as pets in South America. Young cassowaries are also kept as pets in New Guinea. Adults are sometimes kept for their plumage.

△ Ostriches are moved along a highway, like sheep, in South Africa, where they are still raised on farms.

▷ Rheas in a zoo, living in a habitat designed to be like their natural home on the South American pampas.

◁An ostrich guarding
its eggs on a farm in
South Africa. In the wild,
the female watches over
the eggs during the day,
the male at night.

▽An ostrich race
provides entertainment
for visitors to the farm.

△ Ostriches are still plucked for their feathers on farms. This is done without harming them.

▷ Rare flightless birds, like this kakapo being held by a wildlife officer, may be kept in special reserves where they are protected. The kakapo, a ground-dwelling parrot, lives in New Zealand.

The story of flightless birds

Wings not needed

Millions of years ago, some creatures on earth developed wings. They probably started by using their forelimbs to glide down from a tree. Flying enabled them to escape from their enemies. There have been birds on the earth for about 180 million years. For working their wings, they developed powerful muscles, which were anchored to their breastbone by a ridge called a keel.

Over the ages, some birds lost this power of flight. For one reason or another, they were able to live on the ground in safety. It is thought that the large flightless birds of today all evolved in this way. These birds – the ostrich, rhea, emu and cassowary – are often grouped together as "ratites," but they developed separately, probably from different ancestors. What they have in common is powerful legs for running, small wings and the absence of the breastbone keel.

Dead as a dodo

The well-known expression "dead as a dodo" comes from the flightless dodo, a bird that lived on Mauritius, an island in the Indian Ocean. Until this remote island became a stopping place for spice traders in the 1400s, the dodo had no enemies. But sailors began to kill the dodos in their thousands for food, and pigs and monkeys introduced by sailors destroyed their eggs and ate their young. The dodo became extinct in 1680.

The great auk, a flightless penguinlike bird that lived on North Atlantic coasts, met the same fate in the 1840s.

△ The great auk, the only European bird to become extinct in modern times. Like the dodo before it, the great auk disappeared from the earth because of overhunting.

△ The moa, a New Zealand bird that became extinct about 700 years ago, shown (left) dwarfing three kiwis. A skeleton (right) is shown compared with one of a human.

More extinct birds

Many other flightless birds have become extinct for similar reasons – the arrival in their habitat of an enemy, usually the human species. Ratites larger than the ostrich once existed, such as the elephant bird of Madagascar and the greater moa of New Zealand. They died out most probably because of human interference.

Fashionable feathers

In Africa, ostriches were once killed for their feathers. The San, a wandering people of southern Africa, still use ostrich eggshells for storing water. When ostriches populated western Asia hundreds of years ago, they were hunted for sport.

About a hundred years ago, ostrich plumes became very fashionable. They were used for decoration of ladies' hats and clothing. Hunted for its feathers, the ostrich disappeared from Asia and much of Africa. People began to raise ostriches on farms. Their feathers could be plucked twice a year without harming the birds. Ostrich farms were set up in the United States and Australia as well as in Africa. Ostrich feathers later went out of fashion, but there are still farms in South Africa where the birds are raised for their skins.

△ The birds are blindfolded as their plumes are plucked on a Californian ostrich farm in the earlier part of this century.

Facts and records

△ An ostrich egg, the largest of any living bird.

△ An X ray of a kiwi shows its huge egg compared with its own size.

Largest egg

The ostrich lays the largest egg of any living bird. It averages 15–20 cm (6–8 in) long with a weight of 1.7 kg (4 lb).

The largest egg laid, relative to the size of the bird, is the Kiwi egg, which may be as long as 13 cm (5 in).

Tough shell

Although the shell of an ostrich egg is only 1.5 mm (1/16th in) thick, it can support the weight of an adult human.

Fastest

The ostrich is the fastest land bird. It can travel at speeds of 65 km/h (40 mph).

△ An ostrich at full speed.

△ A person can stand on an ostrich egg without breaking the shell.

Glossary

Ancestors
The ancestors of today's birds are the birds or other animals they developed from over millions of years.

Covey
A small group of birds.

Extinct
A species is extinct when there are no longer any living specimens.

Flightless
Unable to fly.

Flipper
A limb that has been adapted for swimming.

Habitat
The natural surroundings in the wild where a particular species lives.

Incubate
To keep an egg warm until it is ready to hatch.

Keel
A ridge along the breastbone of birds that supports the powerful flight muscles. The larger flightless birds do not have this keel.

Nocturnal
Active at night.

Pampas
The grassy plains of South America.

Predator
An animal that preys on another, killing it for food.

Ratite
A name given to the large flightless birds – ostriches, emus, rheas and cassowaries. Although the ratites belong to different families, they have similar features, such as powerful legs, small wings and no keel on their breastbone.

Rookery
Colonies of birds or other animals where they come together for breeding. Penguins gather in rookeries.

Species
A particular kind of animal. Animals of the same species breed young of that species.

Index